Fermenting vol. 2: Fermented Beverages

by Rashelle Johnson

Disclaimer:

This information is provided for consumer informational and educational purposes only and may not reflect the most current information available. This book is sold with the understanding the author and/or publisher is not giving medical advice, nor should the information contained in this book replace medical advice, nor is it intended to diagnose or treat any disease, illness or other medical condition. Always consult your medical practitioner before making any dietary changes or treating or attempting to treat any medical condition.

This information does not cover all possible uses, precautions, interactions or adverse effects of the topics covered in this book. Do not disregard, avoid, or delay seeking medical advice because of something you may have read in this book. Always consult your doctor before adding herbs to your diet or applying them using any of the methods described herein.

While we endeavor to keep the information up to date and correct, we make no representations or warranties of any kind, express or implied, about the completeness, accuracy, reliability, suitability or availability with respect to the book or the information, products, services, or related graphics contained book for any purpose. Any reliance you place on such information is therefore strictly at your own risk.

It's important that you use good judgment when it comes to fermented food. Do not consume food you think may have gone bad bad because it looks, smells or tastes bad. The author claims no responsibility for any liability, loss or damage caused as a result of use of the information found in this book.

Dedication:

This book is dedicated to all those who have discovered the many benefits of fermented food and beverages. I'd like to thank my friends and family, who were kind enough to taste test the recipes for this book. Thanks guys! I couldn't have done it without you.

Contents

What Are Fermented Beverages?

Fermented beverages are naturally cultured beverages made using *lacto-fermenting*, which is a process in which healthy bacteria are used to naturally break down organic food items and beverages, making them healthier to eat and easier to digest in the process.

Fermenting has been in use for thousands of years as a food preservation technique. Foods that normally go bad in a few days or weeks can last months once fermentation has begun. Fermentation is widely believed to have come about as a method of preserving crops for times of scarcity. Along with drying and salting, fermenting was a means through which summer and fall crops could be saved for the harsh winter months where food was difficult to grow or find. Our ancient ancestors didn't know the science behind the fermentation process, but they undoubtedly knew it worked to preserve food and made them healthier in the process.

Fermented beverages use the same lacto-fermentation technique used to preserve food to create tasty probiotic beverages that are full of vitamins, minerals, lactic acid and healthy bacterial flora. These cultured drinks also contain enzymes that aid with digestion and help the body gain as much nutrition as possible from every morsel of food it takes in.

These beverages taste great and are good for your health, standing in stark contrast to many of the drinks sold in grocery stores today. While soda and store-bought fruit juice is packed full of sugar—and who knows what else—you control what goes into your fermented beverages, making them the best choice when you feel like drinking something other than water. You don't have to worry about what you're giving to your family because you have ultimate control over the ingredients. By using organic fruit and vegetables, filtered or distilled water and other all-natural and healthy ingredients, you create a healthy beverage largely free of the chemicals and preservatives found in the drinks sold in stores today. The argument could be made that fermented beverages are better than water, but I'll leave that for you to decide.

What I will tell you is this. If you've been consuming processed foods for years and haven't given much thought to what you're eating, your body may be severely lacking in the probiotic bacteria it needs.

For tens of thousands of years—and possibly longer—the human race consumed large amounts of fermented foods and drank heartily of fermented beverages. The foods we ate and the beverages we drank were alive with healthy bacteria that helped balance the flora levels in our gut. In modern times, in an effort to combat bad bacteria we've largely switched to a diet of pasteurized and processed foods that are virtual dead zones when it comes to bacteria. While the processing kills the bad bacteria as intended, the healthy bacteria don't make it through to the end product either. In our attempt to keep bad bacteria at bay, we're starving our bodies of the good bacteria it needs to thrive.

While it sure isn't the only reason for the decline in overall health seen in recent years, it stands to reason the elimination of good bacteria from our diet could be one of the contributing factors. Fermented foods and beverages add those good bacteria back to your diet.

What Happens During Fermentation?

Fermentation is a natural process through which microorganisms are used to break down food products, converting the carbohydrates in the food into organic acids, alcohol and carbon dioxide. The fermentation process is usually intentionally initiated by introduction of probiotic cultures or the creation of conditions where cultures already present on the food can thrive.

There are two types of microorganisms commonly used in fermentation. Yeast is used to ferment breads and to create alcoholic beverages because it converts the sugars found in food into alcohol. Bacteria are used to ferment a number of foods, including fruits and vegetables, because they convert carbohydrates into acids and carbon dioxide. The most common bacteria in use today are *lacto-bacteria*. Molds can also form during the fermentation process, but are usually a result of oxygen being introduced into the fermentation and are undesirable.

In order for beneficial bacteria to thrive, *anaerobic conditions* are needed. Good bacteria are anaerobic by nature, meaning they don't need oxygen to survive. This stands in stark contrast to most bad bacteria, which need oxygen to survive and grow. By creating anaerobic conditions in which foods and beverages can ferment, harmful bacteria are kept at bay while beneficial bacteria are able to multiply and grow.

The lacto-fermentation process preserves food by preventing the growth of harmful bacteria that cause food to spoil. The healthy organisms take over and start processing the food, creating lactic acid and other beneficial compounds in the process. The lactic acid further preserves the food by blocking the growth of bad bacteria.

72 degrees F is the ideal temperature for fermenting most vegetables and a number of cultured drinks. When a recipe in this book calls for fermenting at room temperature, the ambient temperature of the area the fermenting vessel is placed in should be as close to 72 degrees as possible. Some variation in the temperature is allowed, and fermentation can take place at both hotter and cooler temperatures.

When temperatures are too high, fermentation takes place at a much faster pace. Foods will go soft quickly and problems are more likely to arise because of the speed at which fermentation occurs. Monitor foods fermented at temperatures higher than 72 degrees F closely.

Foods fermented at cooler temperatures than what's ideal will do the exact opposite. The colder the temperature at which the fermenting vessel is stored, the slower the food inside will ferment. If temperatures drop too low, fermentation will grind to a halt. This can allow harmful bacteria to take hold and mold is more likely to form.

Cold can be used to your advantage.

Ferment foods at room temperature until they've fermented to your liking, and then move them to a cooler area like a root cellar or the fridge. The cold will slow the fermenting process down and the food will keep for a lot longer than it would if you left it at room temperature. It's important to note putting food in the fridge won't completely stop fermenting. Food will still ferment and will eventually go soft or get too sour to eat. Chilled fermented foods last longer than foods left at room temperature, but they don't last forever.

Freezing or boiling food will completely stop fermentation, but will kill all of the healthy bacteria in the process. For this reason, cooking fermented foods isn't recommended, especially if you're eating them for their probiotic value.

When it comes to fermented beverages, there is more variation in the temperatures at which they need to be fermented. Whenever special temperatures are needed for fermenting a certain beverage, it'll be mentioned in the chapter for that beverage.

Types of Fermented Drinks

There are a wide variety of fermented beverages in existence, many of which are traditional beverages that make use of products local to the area the drinks are native to. If you come across a recipe in this book that has ingredients you can't source locally, there's a pretty good chance you can find what you need online. Be sure to get the ingredients from a reputable source and always buy organic. You don't want to offset the health value of your fermented drinks by adding pesticides and traces of other chemical elements.

Let's take a quick look at some of the fermented drinks being consumed around the world. We'll cover many of these in-depth later on in the book:

Beer and wine. Let's get one thing out of the way upfront. Yes, beer and wine are fermented drinks. No, they aren't covered in this book, the reason being the end result of the fermenting process for beer and wine creates large amounts of alcohol instead of a healthy probiotic drink. While there's something to be said about a cocktail at the end of a long day, this book covers drinks that contain very little alcohol.

Boza. Known as bouza in some regions and boza in others, this beverage is made by fermenting hulled millet. It uses both yeast and lacto-bacteria in the fermenting process.

Ginger beer. While ginger beer does contain alcohol, it's usually only in trace amounts. It's expensive to buy, but is fairly simple and inexpensive to brew at home.

Kefir. Made traditionally from milk, and more recently from coconut milk, kefir is a thick fermented beverage that is closer in consistency to yogurt than it is to liquid. If you're looking for a tasty fermented drink that's almost a meal in a bottle, kefir may fit the bill. There's also a version of kefir made using water that doesn't require milk or coconut milk.

Lacto-fermented soda. This type of soda has a light fizz and a heavy dose of probiotic cultures. Lacto-fermented sodas are a great alternative to the chemical and sugar-laden sodas sold commercially.

Fermented milk beverages. There are a number of bacterial strains used to ferment milk to create probiotic beverages. Fermented milk beverages offer unique flavors and a number of health benefits, but they aren't without their dangers. E. coli and other pathogens can be found in improperly fermented milk beverages.

Fermented tea. There are a number of traditional tea drinks that are fermented. One of the most well-known is kombucha. This tasty fermented sweet tea originated in China, but has now spread throughout the world. It's packed with active enzymes, amino acids and B-vitamins, making it a great choice for those looking for a healthy fermented tea. The alcohol levels in this beverage are fairly low, typically falling below 1%.

Kvass. Kvass is a traditional Russian beverage that is typically made from fermented bread, flour or beets. It has a strong sour taste because it's packed full of lactic acid.

Starter Cultures

Fermented foods are often *inoculated* with *starter cultures*, which are beneficial cultures added to the fermenting vessel in hopes of jump-starting the fermenting process. The following starter cultures are all commonly used:

- **Kefir.** Kefir grains or powder can be added to fermenting foods to ensure they get off to a good start. Some milk-based drinks allow for reuse of the grains multiple times. Kefir grains can be used multiple times as long as they're kept in good health.
- **Liquid from a previous fermentation.** Save a few tablespoons of brine or liquid from a prior fermentation and add them to a new recipe. The brine should be full of probiotic cultures.
- **Dried cultures.** These cultures usually come in the form of packets you open and dump the contents into the fermenting vessel. Dried cultures have to be activated before they're used, so be sure to read the instructions on the package. Dried cultures work well, but tend to be rather expensive and can take a week or longer to rehydrate to the point they can be used.
- **Probiotic capsules.** These capsules are full of beneficial bacteria. Instead of dropping the entire capsule into the vessel, open the capsule and dump the contents into it.

- **Whey.** This starter culture is made by straining probiotic yogurt or buttermilk through cheesecloth. A quarter cup of whey will get your fermented foods and beverages off to a good start as long as you're able to handle milk products. The lactose is already partially broken down, so foods made with whey tend to be more digestible than pasteurized milk products.

Starter cultures aren't always necessary when fermenting food and drinks. If the food already contains healthy bacteria, it can usually be fermented without adding starter cultures. The fermenting process will take longer, but will be entirely natural, which some people believe allows for maximum growth of beneficial bacteria.

Don't Drink Too Much

Fermented beverages are best when consumed in moderation. These powerful probiotic drinks are so full of healthy compounds, all that's needed are small amounts at a time. While drinking more probably isn't going to do any harm, the recommended dosage for the average adult is 6 ounces. If the beverages are given to children, even less is needed. Be aware that there is almost always at least some alcohol in fermented beverages and use them accordingly.

If you've never consumed probiotic beverages, start small and build from there. When trying something new, it's best to test small amounts and build up to more as your body gets used to it. Try an ounce or two the first day and slowly build up to the dosage you want to consume regularly by adding a quarter ounce to a half ounce each day.

While allergic reactions are rare, they can happen and it's best to find out you're allergic to something when you consume only a small amount as opposed to a large amount.

First-time users can experience negative side-effects when they add fermented beverages to their diet. This can be a mild reaction as the body adjusts to the new bacteria or it can be severe. As bad bacteria die off and are replaced by beneficial bacteria, you might feel run down or under the weather. Those experiencing severe side effects they suspect are associated with fermented beverages should discontinue use and consult with a physician immediately.

For this reason, pregnant woman should not add probiotic beverages to their diet without first consulting their physician.

Some fermented beverages can contain alcohol that's created during fermentation. Natural yeasts found in food and starter cultures break sugar down into alcohol and carbon dioxide gas. The amount of alcohol a drink contains depends on how long it's fermented for and how much yeast and sugar there was to begin with. Generally speaking, the more sugar there is for the yeast to act on, the more alcohol you'll be left with in the final product. Beverages left to ferment for long periods of time are more likely to contain elevated levels of alcohol than those fermented for short periods of time.

Unless you're particularly sensitive to alcohol, the levels found in lacto-fermented beverages are of little concern, as long as you don't drink large amounts of the beverage. Most beverages contain less than 2%, so it would take quite a bit to catch a buzz, let alone get drunk. In the United States, drinks with less than 0.5% alcohol are classified as non-alcoholic and a number of the recipes in this book would likely meet that classification. It's difficult to regulate exactly how much alcohol forms in home ferments, so it's important to exercise caution and avoid drinking large amounts of home-fermented beverages.

Aren't All Bacteria Bad?

Bacteria get a bad rap.

Yes, there are bad bacteria, just like there are bad people. But to assume all bacteria are bad just because there are bad bacteria in existence would be akin to assuming all people are inherently bad because there are bad people running around.

The truth of the matter is the body needs a certain level of bacteria to thrive. The good bacteria found in fermented foods are beneficial to the body in a number of ways. They help the body absorb nutrients and help the digestive system process food as it's eaten. Having healthy levels of good bacteria is key to having a happy and healthy immune system, which in turn leads to better overall health. The body is better-prepared to ward off infections and fight inflammation because it isn't wasting valuable resources fighting problems related to an unhealthy digestive system.

Problems arise when bad bacteria outnumber good bacteria in the body. Bad bacteria crave sugar and send signals to the brain indicating sugar is needed. This can lead to overconsumption of sugary items, which can lead to all sorts of health problems, not the least of which are obesity and diabetes. Good bacteria don't send the same signals to the brain because they don't need large amounts of sugar to survive.

Most of the food we eat has been pasteurized or otherwise processed to kill bad bacteria. The lack of bad bacteria is a good thing, but what isn't good is the fact that all of the good bacteria in the food have been destroyed as well. Consuming dead food with no bacteria leaves the body devoid of the beneficial bacteria and enzymes it needs to efficiently process food. This lack of ability to digest food that's eaten combined with bad bacteria craving sugar may lead to impulse eating and weight gain. More food has to be taken in because the digestive system is less efficient at processing it and you might unknowingly be craving unhealthy foods because of their sugar content.

To answer the question, all bacteria aren't bad. In fact, many bacteria are good and are crucial to ensuring the body stays in good working order. Fermented beverages are packed full of these healthy bacteria and are notably devoid of bad bacteria.

Amazake: The Fermented Rice Drink that Isn't Sake

Amazake is an ancient Japanese fermented beverage made by adding fungus to rice. The fungus, known as *Aspergillus oryzae*, breaks cooked rice down into a sweet beverage as it ferments. It's used as a hangover treatment and is believed to be a healthy beverage by those who consume it regularly.

In order to make amazake, you're going to need rice grains that have been inoculated with the Aspergillus culture. These grains are called *koji* and are available at many health food stores and can be purchased online. Koji is also used to make soy sauce, sake and mirin.

It's important to follow fermenting directions closely because koji will convert the sugars in rice into wine if the rice is allowed to ferment long enough. Amazake is low in alcohol because the fermentation process is stopped in the intermediate stage after the rice has been broken down into sugar, but before it starts to turn into alcohol.

Koji is thought to have the following health benefits:

- **Energy boost.**
- **Full of vitamins and minerals.**
- **Helps the body eliminate toxins.**
- **Improved digestion.**

Unlike most fermented foods and beverages, amazake is sweet and doesn't have the same tart taste people normally associate with fermentation. When amazake is finished fermenting, it's usually fairly thick and has to be watered down before it can be consumed as a beverage.

Amazake Recipe

Amazake is more difficult to make than many of the recipes in this book because it requires heating the ingredients to a certain temperature and holding them there for at least 8 hours. Amazake should not be fermented at room temperature because harmful pathogens can form during fermentation.

Ingredients:

5 cups water

4 cups organic brown rice

1 cup koji

A pinch of sea salt

Directions:

Place the water in a pot and bring it to a boil. Add the salt to the pot and stir it in. Add the brown rice and cook it for an hour.

Lower the heat and/or use a flame diffuser to regulate the heat of the pot. Alternatively, place the pot into a large skillet and place the skillet over the burner on the stove. Some people make amazake in their Crockpot or with a dehydrator. No matter the method used, bring the heat of the contents of the pot to between 130 and 140 degrees F and keep it there. Any hotter and you run the risk of killing the bacteria on the koji. Any cooler and you run the risk of harmful pathogens developing. In the required range for at least 12 hours, stirring the contents every couple hours.

After 12 hours, taste the amazake. If it tastes and smells sweet, it's done fermenting.

Amazake has a short shelf life and needs to be consumed quickly. If you're planning on keeping it for more than a day or two, freeze it or bring it to a boil to end the fermentation process. The problem with doing this is it kills all of the probiotic bacteria. If you're looking to get a probiotic boost, consume the amazake shortly after fermenting it without boiling or freezing it first.

Amazake is lumpy and thick when it's done fermenting. Place a cup of amazake in a blender with a cup of hot water and blend it together to get a sweet beverage that can be sipped on or added to smoothies or other drinks as a natural sweetener.

Boza: The (Possibly) Breast-Enhancing Beer

Boza is also known as *bouza* or *bosa*, depending on where in the world you are when you drink it. This traditional drink dates back thousands of years and is popular in most Soviet Bloc countries.

It's a low-alcohol beverage that usually clocks in at somewhere around 1% alcohol content. Boza is classified as a malt drink because it's made from fermented cereal grains that have been germinated and dried partway through the germination process. The type of grain used to produce boza varies from country to country. The following grains are commonly used:

- **Barley.**
- **Buckwheat.**
- **Bulgur.**
- **Maize.**
- **Millet.**
- **Oats.**
- **Rye.**
- **Wheat.**

Some literature refers to boza as boza beer, but that's quite a stretch, considering most beers clock in at 5 to 8 percent alcohol. It would take at least 5 cups of average boza to equal 1 cup of beer in alcohol content.

Boza is a thick, filling beverage packed with lactic acid, vitamins and minerals. It's often used as a meal replacement because you won't feel like eating after drinking a cup of boza.

A single cup of boza contains between 150 and 175 calories, 40 grams of carbohydrates and 3 grams of protein. It's a low-fat beverage, but like many beverages that are low in fat it tends to be high in sugar. You can leave a lot of the sugar out, but you'll be left with a drink that tastes sour instead of sweet. Boza is thought to stimulate lactation, so it's often consumed by women who have just given birth.

Consume boza immediately after fermenting. It can be stored in a cool area for a short period of time, but doesn't keep for long. Drink it within a couple days of moving it to the fridge for best results.

Here's an interesting aside about boza. In some countries it's sold as a breast-enhancing drink. Men purchase it for their wives and girlfriends in hopes it'll enlarge their breasts. For the record, this hasn't been scientifically proven, but it could be a good way for wives and girlfriends to get their significant others to brew up a batch. For the record, I'm living proof it doesn't always work. My breasts haven't increased in size since I started drinking boza.

Maybe I need to drink more . . .

Simple Boza

This quick and easy boza recipe can be made using items you probably already have in your kitchen or pantry. Try topping it with cinnamon and roasted chickpeas for added flavor.

Boza Ingredients:

10 cups of water

1 cup flour

1 cup sugar

1 cup of flour ferment (see below)

Cinnamon (for topping)

Flour Ferment Ingredients:

1 cup lukewarm water

1 tablespoon flour

1 tablespoon dry active yeast

1 tablespoon sugar

Directions:

Toast the flour by placing it on a cookie sheet and baking it until it turns a light pink color. Watch it closely and stir it constantly to avoid burning the flour. Remove one tablespoon for the flour ferment and store the rest of the toasted flour in an airtight container while waiting for the flour ferment to form.

Take a tablespoon of the toasted flour and mix it with a cup of lukewarm water and a tablespoon of sugar. Stir in a tablespoon of dry active yeast. Let the mixture ferment in a warm area of the house for a couple days. Keep it in a glass container covered with cheesecloth while it ferments. Stir the contents at least once a day.

After a couple days have passed, it's time to make the boza. Place 10 cups of water in a pot and bring it to a boil. Stir in the toasted flour and sugar. Let the contents of the pot boil for 6 to 8 minutes, stirring constantly. Remove the pot from the heat and let it cool.

Add the flour ferment to the pot and stir it in. Alternatively, you can use a cup of boza if you have one available. This will speed up the process because you won't have to wait for the flour ferment.

You now have boza that's ready to be fermented. Pour the boza into a glass container and cover the container with cheesecloth or loosely cap it. Keep the boza in a warm place in your house for a few days until it starts to ferment. Once fermentation begins, move the boza to a glass bottle and store it in your fridge. Add cinnamon to the top before serving.

Traditional Boza Recipe

This traditional recipe uses millet flour to create a no-frills boza drink similar to the one that's been in use for thousands of years. If you're looking to experience boza as it tasted when our ancient ancestors consumed it, this is the recipe to try. This recipe does contain alcohol, usually in the range of 1.0% to 2.0% alcohol by volume.

Boza Ingredients:

10 cups of water

1 cup plus 1 tablespoon millet flour

1 cup of sugar

1 cup of millet ferment (see below)

Cinnamon (for topping)

Millet Ferment Ingredients:

1 cup lukewarm water

1 tablespoon millet flour

1 teaspoon sugar

Directions:

Toast the millet flour by placing it in a dry skillet over medium heat and stirring it with a whisk until the flour lightly browns. This should take 6 to 8 minutes. Alternatively, you can spread the flour out on a cookie sheet and toast it in an oven set to 350 degrees F. Toast it for 6 minutes, turning the flour using a whisk at the 3 minute mark.

Create the millet ferment by combining the millet ferment ingredients in a glass bowl and stirring them together. The yeast is optional, but will speed up the fermenting process. Pour the contents of the bowl into a glass container and loosely place the lid on it. Place the container in a warm area of your house and let it ferment for a couple days. Remove the lid and stir the contents of the container at least once a day.

If you have boza left over from a previous ferment, you can use it in place of the millet ferment. A cup of boza works every bit as well as a cup of millet ferment with the added bonus of not having to wait a couple days for the millet ferment to be ready.

Wait a couple days for the millet ferment to start fermenting. At the end of the second day (or on the third day), add the 10 cups of water to a pot and bring the water to a boil. Stir in the millet flour and the sugar. Boil it for 6 to 8 minutes. Do not add the millet ferment or leftover boza while the water is hot.

Remove the pot from the stove and wait for the liquid inside to cool to room temperature. Once it is cool, add the millet ferment to the pot and stir it in. Pour the ferment into a glass container and let it ferment for 2 to 3 days. Once it starts fermenting, move it to the fridge. Serving size is 1 cup. Sprinkle cinnamon on top before drinking.

Bulgur Boza

Bulgur boza is made from *bulgur wheat*, which is a nutty wheat made by partially boiling and sun-drying durum wheat. You probably aren't going to find bulgur wheat on your local grocery store's shelves, unless you have a well-stocked health food store nearby. It can also be found in stores or marketplaces that cater to people of Middle Eastern descent.

Boza Ingredients:

10 cups water

1 cup bulgur

½ cup yogurt

¼ cup of sugar

3 tablespoons flour

1 teaspoon dry active yeast

1 teaspoon vanilla

Cinnamon and sugar, to taste

Directions:

Place the bulgur and 10 cups of water in a large pot and let it soak overnight. Place the pot on the stove over low heat and cook the grains until they are very soft. This usually takes 2 to 3 hours. Remove the pot from the heat and mash the bulgur with a blunt object. Alternatively, the bulgur can be blended in a blender or food processor.

Press the bulgur through a colander and discard any large pieces or pulp left in the strainer. Alternatively, you can boil the larger pieces again and pass them through the strainer if you don't want them to go to waste.

Add ½ cup water to a saucepan over low heat and stir the flour into it. Cook it until it starts to thicken, stirring the entire time. Once the flour thickens, remove it from the heat and immediately stir in the sugar. Let the contents of the saucepan cool. While you're waiting for it to cool, add the yeast to ½ cup warm water and let it sit until the contents of the saucepan have cooled. Once the water and flour in the saucepan has cooled, stir the yogurt and the yeast water into it.

Let the saucepan sit for 30 to 45 minutes.

Combine the yeast flour mixture and the bulgur and blend it together. Place the boza in a glass container and cover the container with cheesecloth or cap it loosely. Let the boza sit for 2 to 3 days. Once it starts to ferment, move it to the fridge. Stir the vanilla in right before serving it. Add cinnamon and sugar, to taste.

Cultured Dairy Drinks

Cultured dairy drinks, also known as *fermented milk drinks*, are made by fermenting milk using various forms of beneficial bacteria. The fermentation process preserves the milk, increasing the shelf life while changing the taste, texture and viscosity. The milk gets thicker and takes on other characteristics that are dependent on the variety of bacteria used. The lacto-bacteria in these cultured dairy drinks help slow spoilage by preventing pathogens from taking over.

Fermented dairy drinks are easier for the human body to digest because the lactose is already partially broken down into its subcomponents. Since lactose is the part of milk lactose-intolerant people have trouble with, cultured dairy products are often easier for those who have problems with lactose to digest. Fermentation also breaks down the casein protein found in dairy, which is one of the more difficult proteins for the body to digest.

Creating a batch of a fermented milk drink requires having the correct starter culture on hand. You add the culture to the milk, place the milk in a glass vessel and place the vessel in an area that's the appropriate temperature. A day or two later the fermented milk drink is alive with probiotic cultures of the strain(s) found in the starter culture.

Once you've made the first batch, new batches of most cultured dairy drinks can be made using a cup of milk saved from the previous batch to inoculate the next batch.

The first batch can be used to make the second batch. The second batch can be used to make the third batch, and so on. This can go on indefinitely as long as you don't wait too long between batches.

It's important that containers and utensils used to create fermented milk beverages are sterilized before use. Boil both the containers and the utensils beforehand to kill off any pathogens they may be harboring. You want to grow healthy bacteria, not bacteria that could make you sick or even kill you. Don't use antibacterial soaps or cleaning products because they can inhibit the growth of healthy bacteria.

Acidophilus Milk

Also known probiotic milk, *acidophilus milk* is sold commercially in a number of states. It's rapidly gaining in popularity, so keep an eye out for it in your local grocery store. If it hasn't hit grocery store shelves in your area yet, check health food stores in your area. Failing that, you can always make it yourself at home.

Acidophilus milk gets its name because it contains the *lactobacillus acidophilus* bacteria. This bacteria strain gives acidophilus milk a tart taste and thickens the milk up to where it's close the viscosity of yogurt, but is thin enough to be pourable. This low-fat fermented milk drink has a distinctly sour taste. If left to ferment for too long, acidophilus milk can get pretty sour. Try adding honey or vanilla to it before you consume it to mask the flavor.

Acidophilus milk is low-fat and doesn't contain the same levels of lactose regular milk has in it. Since it's only lightly fermented, it will still contain some lactose, making it a bad choice for people who are strongly lactose intolerant. The probiotic cultures in the milk aid with digestion and some believe they help ease the effects of allergies. There are studies that appear to indicate acidophilus bacteria block absorption of cholesterol, which may help lower bad cholesterol levels.

This fermented beverage isn't for everyone.

Some people report bloating, gas and other digestive issues when they consume acidophilus milk, especially if they drink large amounts. The initial discomfort is often short-lived, but acidophilus milk should be avoided by those who are allergic to milk.

Acidophilus Milk Recipe

For those who can't find it (or who want to avoid paying the steep price), acidophilus milk can be made at home. You're going to need a live acidophilus culture. You can find acidophilus cultures online or at a local health food store. Plain yogurt that contains live cultures can be used as long as the label says it has lactobacillus acidophilus in it.

Ingredients:

1 gallon milk

1 cup yogurt (containing acidophilus cultures)

Food thermometer

Directions:

Sterilize the containers you plan on using to make the milk. Add the milk to a large covered pot and scald it, bringing the temperature of the milk up to 190 degrees F. Don't let the milk boil, as it will change the flavor and chemical composition of the milk.

Remove the pot from the heat and let the milk cool to between 90 and 105 degrees F before adding the starter culture. If you're using a packet of starter culture, cool it to the temperature stated on the starter culture packet. Be careful not to add the starter culture while the milk is too hot because it will kill the bacteria. Cooling can be sped up by placing the pot full of milk in a cool water bath.

Stir the cultures into the pot of milk when the temperature reaches 105 degrees F unless the cultures came with instructions that state otherwise.

Pour the milk into sterile glass containers. Place a lid on each container and screw it down tightly. The milk needs to be kept between 90 and 105 degrees F for the next 24 hours. This can be done in a number of ways. A yogurt maker is the easiest because all you do is place the jars in the yogurt maker and set the temperature.

If you don't have a yogurt maker, you can use your oven. Most ovens don't have a setting for the low temperatures needed for acidophilus milk, so you're going to have to innovate. Turn the oven on to a higher setting until it heats to 110 degrees F. Turn the oven off when it reaches the desired temperature. Place the containers of milk into the oven and close it. The temperatures inside the oven should stay in the range you need for at least 12 hours. Check the temperature every 6 hours and turn the oven on again to reheat the inside to the proper temperature if you need to.

Check the milk each time you check the temperature to see if it has soured to your liking. If it has, move it to the fridge. If not, continue fermenting it in your oven, checking on it every couple hours. If you let acidophilus milk ferment for too long, it turns into yogurt. This isn't necessarily a bad thing, but you won't be able to drink it like a beverage.

Amasi

Amasi is a fermented milk drink of African descent. This drink is known for its ability to help the body break down the proteins contained in the milk it's made from and is packed full of lacto-bacteria and healthy microorganisms that aid in digestion and the absorption of nutrients. When you consider the benefits, it's no wonder amasi is consumed by people of all walks of life in Africa. From Masai warriors to businessmen working in the big cities, amasi is a favorite beverage.

This beverage came about as a means of preserving milk long before refrigeration was an option. The lactic acid in amasi helps protect it from harmful pathogens like E. coli. Amasi is at its best when made from raw milk obtained from grass-fed cows. While raw milk is easily sourced in Africa, restrictive rules and regulations have made it difficult to obtain in the United States. Short of owning a grass-fed dairy cow or knowing someone who does, it may be all but impossible to obtain the raw milk needed for this fermented drink in heavily regulated states.

Some people claim amasi is similar in taste and texture to plain yogurt. Some say it tastes similar to cottage cheese. Others say it tastes horrible and is all but impossible to drink. Most people either love it or hate it. It's normally consumed as a beverage, but is also added to some foods and served over grain.

Amasi is made by taking full cream raw milk, adding amasi to it and placing it in a container. The container is then left to sit out for a day or two. The milk separates and the amasi is collected. The problem with making amasi is you need to use amasi as a starter culture.

Be aware that harmful bacteria can form in amasi during the fermentation process. If commercial amasi is available in your area, you can buy it. If not, you may be able to order it online. Those who can't find it commercially are better off making one of the less risky fermented beverages in this book.

Buttermilk

Buttermilk is a drink that takes many forms. Some people refer to any soured milk recipe as buttermilk. Many of the fermented milk beverages in this chapter have been called buttermilk by those who make and drink them. It's somewhat of a generic term used to refer to fermented milk drinks.

There are two main types of buttermilk.

They share the name *buttermilk*, but have little else in common other than they're both a milk product. *Traditional buttermilk* is the liquid left behind when cream is churned into butter. It's the viscosity of regular milk and has little pieces of butter floating in it. *Cultured buttermilk* is made by introducing either *lactobacillus bulgaricus* or *streptococcus lactis* bacteria into cow's milk and letting it ferment. It's thick and creamy and has a distinctly tart flavor.

The bacteria introduced into buttermilk process the lactose found in the milk, creating lactic acid as a byproduct. The lactic acid is what gives buttermilk its distinctly sour flavor and is the reason why buttermilk has an extended shelf life in comparison to regular milk. Buttermilk is thicker than regular milk in consistency because the casein in buttermilk has precipitated.

The high levels of lactic acid in buttermilk give it a long shelf life when it's refrigerated. Buttermilk can last for as long as a month in the fridge before it starts to go bad. While it's OK to drink, older buttermilk shouldn't be used to inoculate new batches of buttermilk because the cultures may have died off. It's best to use buttermilk that's less than 2 weeks old to inoculate new batches.

Cultured Buttermilk Recipe

This recipe is for cultured buttermilk, which is the most common type of buttermilk made today. It's made by adding active buttermilk cultures to whole milk. For thinner buttermilk, try 2% or even skim milk.

Ingredients:

1 cup active cultured buttermilk

4 cups whole milk

Directions:

Purchase a container of active cultured buttermilk. This shouldn't be too hard to find. Most grocery stores carry active cultured buttermilk. Try to find a new container that hasn't been sitting on the shelf for a long time. The closer the buttermilk is to its expiration date, the fewer active cultures it's going to have.

Add 1 cup of active cultured buttermilk to 4 cups of whole milk. Stir the buttermilk into the whole milk and pour the mixture into a glass jar. Place the lid tightly on the jar and let the jar sit at room temperature for 24 hours. Check the buttermilk to see if it has clabbered. If not, let it sit for another 12 hours. If it hasn't clabbered by this point, throw out the batch and try again with new buttermilk.

Move the finished buttermilk to the fridge.

Once you've made a batch of buttermilk, you can use a cup of buttermilk from your old batch to make the next batch as long as it isn't too old. As long as you stay on top of things, you can continue making new batches using buttermilk from the previous batch indefinitely.

Traditional Buttermilk Recipe

This recipe doesn't just make buttermilk. It makes butter, too.

Buttermilk is technically just a byproduct of the butter churning process. For some reason, there's a general misconception that making butter at home is difficult. Sure, churning it by hand is a bit of work, but you don't have to churn butter manually unless you want to. An electric blender or mixer can be used to make butter the easy way, without wearing out your arms.

This recipe calls for using a blender. A stand mixer can be used to make larger amounts of butter and buttermilk. When using a stand mixer, make sure you cover the mixing bowl or buttermilk will splatter everywhere. Once you've decided how you're going to churn your butter, all 're going to need to make butter and traditional buttermilk is cream. If you want salted butter, you're also going to need a bit of sea salt.

Ingredients:

High quality cream

Sea salt (optional)

Directions:

You're going to need good cream to make good butter. The best cream is organic cream from grass-fed cows. Pour the cream into the blender and blend it on high until the butter starts to separate. As soon as you see the butter separating, stop the blender and let it sit for 5 minutes.

The butter will rise to the top and the liquid buttermilk will be beneath it. Pour the buttermilk into a glass container. Use a blunt object to compress the butter and squeeze as much buttermilk out of it as you can. The buttermilk in the container is traditional buttermilk.

Keep the container refrigerated until the buttermilk is used.

The next step is rinsing the butter. This step is optional, but should be done if you won't use the butter right away. Rinsing removes the milk from the butter in an effort to prolong shelf life. Pour a cup of ice cold water into the blender and blend the butter for another minute. Dump the water out and press the butter again to get any buttermilk that's left out of it.

If you're planning on adding sea salt, now's the time to do it. Stir it into the butter. Package the butter in an airtight container. The butter can be kept at room temperature if you're planning on using it quickly. It will last longer if it's stored in the fridge, so move it to the fridge if you don't plan on using it right away.

<u>Chaas</u>

Chaas is an Indian drink made from yogurt, sour milk or buttermilk. This recipe uses cultured buttermilk and is an absolutely delicious blend of buttermilk and spices. Serve it chilled as a mid-day snack to provide energy for the rest of the day. This recipe makes 1 cup of chaas.

Ingredients:

1 cup cultured buttermilk

½ teaspoon cumin seed powder

¼ teaspoon diced green chilies

A pinch of black pepper

Sea salt, to taste

Roasted cumin seeds, to taste

Water (optional)

Directions:

Combine all of the ingredients in a glass bowl and whisk together. If you want a thinner beverage, add water until the chaas is the consistency you want it to be. Serve in a glass with ice.

Filmjölk

Filmjölk is a fermented milk product that's cultured at room temperature. It's a Nordic breakfast beverage that is made in a manner similar to yogurt, but uses different bacteria in the fermentation process. Filmjölk can be drunk, but it's often eaten with a spoon because it tends to be rather thick. Sugary fruit, jams, jellies and honey are often added to offset the slightly sour taste. It tastes closer to cheese than it does traditional yogurt, but is closer in consistency to yogurt than it is cheese.

Lactococcus lactis and *leuconostoc mesenteroides* bacteria strains are used to make filmjölk. These bacteria act on the lactose in the milk, converting it to lactic acid. This gives the filmjölk a sour flavor. Diacetyl is also formed, which adds a slight buttery flavor to the drink.

To make filmjölk, you're going to need filmjölk cultures.

A tablespoon or two of filmjölk from a previous batch is typically added to pasteurized milk, which is then left to sit in a warm area of the house for up to a day. If you don't have access to filmjölk, you can purchase filmjölk starter. The good news is you'll probably only have to buy it once. As long as you save some of the filmjölk from the previous batch, you can use it to culture the next batch. This can be continued indefinitely.

The first batch may need to be cultured for up to 48 hours. It can take cultures a little longer to get going at first. If the first batch or two aren't strong enough, toss them out and continue making batches until they're to your liking.

Follow the directions that come with the starter cultures to create your first batch of filmjölk. Once you have the first batch made, making the next batch is as simple as adding a tablespoon of filmjölk from your previous batch for every cup of pasteurized milk you add to the next batch. If you use 1 cup of milk, you'd add 1 tablespoon of filmjölk. 2 cups of milk would get 2 tablespoons of filmjölk, and so on.

Cover the jar with cheesecloth or a towel and secure the cover in place. Let the jar sit for 12 hours. Check it and move it to the fridge if it's jelled. The filmjölk will set when it's ready. If not, let it sit for another 6 hours and check it again. If the curds separate from the whey, the temperature of the contents of the container was probably too warm during fermentation. Try to keep the temperature in the range of 70 to 75 degrees F.

When using an old batch to inoculate a new batch, a new batch should be made every 5 to 7 days. If you wait longer than that, there may not be enough active cultures in the previous batch to jump-start the new batch. The more fat there is in the milk you use, the thicker the filmjölk will be. Whole milk will turn into filmjölk that needs to be eaten with a spoon. Low fat milk will make thinner filmjölk that can be consumed as a beverage.

Matsoni

If you're looking for an easy to make fermented milk product that is made at room temperature, *matsoni* fits the bill. Matsoni is an Eastern European cultured dairy beverage thought by those who consume it to promote longevity. It's typically consumed at breakfast and tastes great combined with yogurt and fruit.

Matsoni has a slightly cheesy flavor and a creamy consistency. It's one of the few fermented milk beverages kids will tolerate. Try adding honey or sweet fruit preserves to matsoni to further mask the taste. My son is convinced strawberry preserves combined with matsoni tastes just like the Danimals yogurt he loves.

Most people don't like the flavor of matsoni on its own, but it works well when added to smoothies or with fruit added to it.

The probiotic bacteria in matsoni include *lactobacillus delbrueckii* and *streptococcus thermophiles*, which are both good bacteria for a normal person to have in their digestive system. They help the body digest food and are key in slowing the growth of harmful bacteria.

Matsoni is used in a number of traditional dishes. Remember that any dish that bakes or otherwise cooks the matsoni will kill off the bacterial cultures.

Matsoni Recipe

You need two ingredients to make matsoni: the correct starter culture and milk. Grocery stores that cater to Eastern Europeans often carry matsoni and matsoni cultures. Matsoni starter culture can be ordered online if you aren't able to source it locally.

Ingredients:

½ cup matsoni starter culture

8 cups whole milk

Directions:

Combine the matsoni starter culture with 8 cups of whole milk and whisk together. Place the milk in a large glass container and cover it loosely.

Let the milk sit for 6 hours at room temperature and check it to if it has set. The ideal temperature to cultivate matsoni is between 70 and 80 degrees F. The matsoni will be the consistency of syrup when it's ready. Check it every 6 hours to see if it has set.

It should take less than 24 hours.

Once the matsoni has set, bottle it and store it in the fridge until you're ready to drink it.

Piimä

Like filmjölk, *piimä* is cultured dairy beverage of Scandinavian origin. It also tastes like cheese, but leans more toward the sour side. Piimä isn't as thick as most cultured milk beverages and is easy to drink. It's similar in viscosity and flavor to buttermilk and makes for a tasty addition to smoothies and breakfast beverages.

Preparing your first batch of piimä requires having access to another batch of piimä or piimä starter culture. Once you've created one batch of piimä, you can continue making piimä indefinitely.

To make piimä, add a tablespoon of piimä for each cup of milk you're using in your recipe. If you're using starter culture, follow the instructions that came with it. Set it out at room temperature in a glass container covered by a towel or cheesecloth and let it ferment for 12 hours. Once it sets, move it to the fridge.

Piimä Cream

This thick cream is similar enough in taste and texture to sour cream that it can be used to replace it in pretty much any recipe that calls for sour cream. I use piimä cream quite a bit while cooking and have never noticed much of a difference. Be aware that heating the piimä cream will kill the probiotic bacteria.

Ingredients:

1 tablespoon piimä

1 cup heavy cream

Directions:

Combine a tablespoon of piimä with a cup of heavy whipping cream and blend it together to create a great sour cream replacement.

Piimä Dressing

Here's a salad dressing you can use to add probiotic bacteria to your diet. This dressing goes well with garden salads and leafy greens. It can also be used as a vegetable dip to good effect.

Ingredients:

1 cup piimä

½ cup mayonnaise

1 garlic clove, minced

2 teaspoons extra virgin olive oil

1 tablespoon dried dill

½ teaspoon garlic salt

½ teaspoon oregano

Salt and pepper, to taste

Directions:

Place the ingredients in a blender and blend them until the dressing is a smooth consistency.

Piimä Fruit Smoothie

This recipe is for a piimä strawberry smoothie. It can just as easily be used in other smoothies. Substitute your favorite preserves for the strawberry preserves used in this recipe.

Ingredients:

1 cup piimä

5 ice cubes

4 to 6 tablespoons strawberry preserves

5 strawberries

Raw honey, to taste

Directions:

Add all of the ingredients to a blender and blend until smooth. Drink immediately.

Kefir

Kefir is a fermented beverage made by introducing kefir grains to either milk or water and letting them ferment. Milk kefir is the more popular choice world-wide, but in recent years water kefir has established itself as a popular fermented beverage amongst those who are sensitive to dairy or are looking to eliminate dairy from their diet.

Milk kefir is typically made using animal milk, with cow's milk being the number one milk of choice. Goat milk is also popular. In recent years, variations of milk kefir using coconut milk have sprouted up and are a great choice for those looking to cut dairy out of their diet. *Water kefir* eschews dairy altogether, instead using water or some form of fruit juice.

Kefir, regardless of whether it's made with water or milk, is packed full of a wide variety of beneficial bacteria and yeasts. There are more than 400 different strains of yeast and bacteria known to grow in kefir. The exact amount and type of bacteria and yeast found in an individual kefir strain depends on the kefir grains it was cultured from and the environment in which the kefir was fermented.

There are a handful of key differences between milk kefir and water kefir. Milk kefir is more nutritious, as it has similar health benefits to milk. Water kefir isn't as nutritious, but it is less fattening because it's made with water as opposed to milk that contains milk fat. Both water and milk kefir contain probiotic bacteria. The type of bacteria found in each is different, but there are large amounts of probiotic bacteria in both drinks.

All About Kefir Grains

The first thing most people think of when they hear the term "kefir grains" are cereal grains like rye, wheat, oats or barley. Imagine their surprise when the kefir grains arrive on their doorstep and they look more like soft cauliflower florets. Kefir grains are off-white to white in color and are soft to the touch, which makes them almost the exact opposite of most cereal grains. They range in size from the size of a grain of rice to 4" to 5" across.

Healthy kefir grains will be white to off-white in color and range from being tightly coiled to looking like long ribbons. The look of kefir grains can change over time and it isn't unheard of for kefir grains to stretch out when in warmer weather. It's difficult to tell whether kefir grains are healthy just by looking at them. Most people consider their kefir grains healthy as long as they're able to produce good kefir with them.

Kefir grains aren't all built the same. They differ from grain to grain and all kefir grains change over time. They take on characteristics of the environment in which they're used and no two kefir strains are exactly the same. There are more than 400 yeasts and bacterial cultures known to exist in kefir grains and there are undoubtedly more that haven't been discovered. For this reason, no two batches of kefir will be exactly the same.

If you culture kefir too close to other fermenting foods or beverages it may take on some of the bacteria growing in the other containers. This tendency to change is both a bane and boon. You never know exactly what you're going to get when you ferment a new batch, so be prepared to be surprised. Sometimes the surprises are good, while other times, you might not be pleased with the change. That's the nature of kefir and there isn't much you can do about it.

To keep kefir grains healthy, they have to constantly be fed.

Think of kefir grains as a living, breathing entity and treat them accordingly. Neglected kefir grains don't produce good kefir, if they produce at all. It's best to move kefir to new milk every 24 hours. If you aren't able to consume the kefir you're making fast enough to sustain this pace, place the kefir grains in milk and place them in the fridge. This will allow you to wait a week before you have to change the milk.

You can also dry kefir grains at room temperature and store them for up to 6 months. Dry grains will have to be reactivated by placing them in milk and swapping the milk out every 24 hours until they're producing good kefir.

Kefir grains prefer to be used on the same type of liquid each time they're used. Liquid types can be switched, but it may take a handful of batches for the kefir to acclimate to the new milk. The speed at which kefir grains ferment the liquid they're in can vary, with some grains taking their sweet time while others rapidly ferment any liquid they're dropped in.

Milk kefir grains are different from water kefir grains. There are cases where people have got milk kefir grains to acclimate to fermenting water or juice, but it's best to use milk kefir grains to ferment milk and water kefir grains to ferment other liquids.

There's neither rhyme nor reason to it, but you may find your kefir is growing in size or there are new grains popping up in your kefir. This is normal behavior, but don't be concerned if you don't see new grains. Some kefir cultures prolifically create baby kefir grains, while others rarely grow.

If kefir grains grow too large, they can be broken apart. If you're having trouble getting your grains to work and they're starting to develop a crust on them, it sometimes helps if you put them in the blender or grab a knife and chop them up. This can help revitalize stressed grains that have stopped growing and are no longer producing kefir.

If left for too long without food or placed under too much stress, kefir grains can die. If this happens, there's nothing you can do to bring them back to life. You'll have to start over with new kefir grains. Treat your kefir grains like they're a pet and feed them regularly and you may find your kefir grains last a lifetime.

Milk Kefir

Milk kefir is an effervescent probiotic beverage made using whole or powdered milk kefir grains to ferment some form of animal milk. It can be made from almost any type of milk, but prefers milk with a lot of fat in it. Ultra-pasteurized milk is difficult to produce kefir from because of the process through which the milk is pasteurized.

Kefir grains are probiotic cultures made of a combination of lacto-bacteria and various yeasts packed into a cauliflower-shaped chunk of fats, sugars and proteins. Milk kefir is made by adding milk kefir grains to milk and allowing the milk to ferment at or near room temperature. Kefir grains are in a constant state of growth and the flavor and texture of the kefir they produce tends to change over time. This is one of the nuances of kefir and is unavoidable.

Milk kefir tastes like lightly carbonated soda mixed with cream. It's effervescent and has a light tang to it. While some fermented milk drinks are difficult to drink for those new to fermented drinks, most people like milk kefir when it's mixed with honey and/or fruit.

Unlike many other fermented beverages, the temperature at which kefir ferments isn't critical, as long as it isn't above 100 degrees F or below 39 degrees F. Ideally, fermentation will take place in an area with an ambient temperature around 74 degrees F. At this temperature, milk kefir will take between 12 and 24 hours to properly ferment. If it's cooler, fermenting will take longer. Warmer temperatures will speed the process up and the likelihood of the kefir separating into curds and whey increases.

Milk kefir grains will often form as part of the fermentation process. These grains can be filtered from the milk kefir. Dry them at room temperature and save them for future batches of kefir. Milk kefir grains make it through the fermenting process largely intact, as long as they are strained out before the 48-hour mark. Grains can be used over and over again to produce new batches of milk kefir. Powdered milk kefir grains can only be used once, but you may be able to use kefir from one batch to inoculate another.

There are a number of health benefits associated with milk kefir. Here are just some of the many beneficial qualities kefir is thought to have:

- **Adds beneficial bacteria and yeast to the digestive tract.**
- **Aids digestion.**
- **Combats gastrointestinal distress.**
- **Contains vitamins and minerals.**
- **Fights inflammation.**
- **May have anticancer properties.**
- **May help manage free radicals.**
- **May reduce blood pressure and cholesterol.**
- **Wards off pathogens.**

The fermenting process for milk kefir creates a small amount of alcohol. The percentage is usually low; with most batches ending up between 0.5% and 2% alcohol by volume. Generally speaking, kefir allowed to ferment for longer periods of time will have more alcohol than kefir fermented for short periods of time at the optimal fermenting temperature.

Simple Milk Kefir Recipe

While milk kefir sounds and tastes like an exotic beverage, it's easy to make once you have the milk kefir grains in hand. If you know someone who produces milk kefir locally, ask them if they can spare a few grains. If not, milk kefir grains can be purchased online. Milk kefir made using this recipe can be used in any recipe that calls for milk kefir, including the rest of the recipes in this chapter.

Ingredients:

2 teaspoons milk kefir grains

2 cups of milk

Directions:

If you're making this recipe for the first time using newly purchased dried kefir grains, follow the instructions on the package to rehydrate the grains. Once the grains have been rehydrated (or if you're using grains that have already been used to make kefir), place 2 teaspoons of milk kefir grains into 2 cups of milk. Keep in mind the amount of kefir grains needed can vary. You might find you only need 1 teaspoon of grains or you might find you need 3. You might also find a teaspoon or two of the kefir grains you have can ferment 4 or more cups of milk. Generally speaking, kefir grains get stronger over time, so start small and build from there. The more kefir grains you use, the stronger the kefir will be.

Stir the milk and grains using a wooden spoon. The kefir grains will not dissolve into the milk, but stirring helps disperse bacteria into the milk.

Place the kefir grains and milk in a glass jar and place a towel or cheesecloth over the top of the jar and secure it tightly. Leave about a quarter of the jar empty to account for expansion. You want to allow for a bit of air circulation in the jar. Tie the towel or cheesecloth to the jar, so it won't fall off. Place the jar in a dark area of your home that's as close to 74 degrees F as possible. Check it every 12 hours.

After 24 hours have passed, strain out the kefir grains and move them to a fresh container of milk. The kefir you took the grains from can be left to ferment at room temperature for another 24 hours to continue fermenting if you want it to ferment more. Letting kefir ferment for another day increases the lactic acid content and decreases the lactose in the kefir.

Do not use a tight lid while fermenting kefir. A lot of pressure can build up in the container, which can cause the lid to pop off violently. Containers under pressure have been known to explode, so make sure any pressure that builds up in the container is able to escape.

Once the milk thickens, remove the kefir grains by straining the kefir through a 1/8" strainer. Kefir usually starts to thicken at the top of the container and moves down, so be sure to check the bottom of the container to make sure it's set.

When it's done, move the milk kefir to the fridge. If the milk tastes strongly of yeast, try using fewer kefir grains with the next batch. If the kefir doesn't take hold within 48 hours, discard the milk and try again.

Fizzy Kefir

Milk kefir is only lightly carbonated when you first move it to the fridge. This technique can be used to make kefir fizzier, like a carbonated soda.

Ingredients:

Freshly fermented milk kefir

A bottle with a rubber seal

Directions:

As soon as your kefir is done fermenting, move it to an airtight bottle. The bottle should have a lid with a rubber seal on it to prevent it from exploding from the pressure. Tightly seal the lid and leave the kefir to sit in a warm area of your house for an additional day or two. This will cause carbonation to build up in the kefir, making it fizzier.

Open the lid at least once a day to release the pressure building up inside. Once the kefir is fizzy enough, drink it or move it to the fridge.

Coconut Milk Kefir

Many people who are lactose intolerant are able to tolerate milk kefir because the proteins and lactose in the dairy are already partially broken down. For those who still can't handle it (or don't want dairy in their diet), coconut kefir is a good option. Be aware that a small amount of milk will make its way into the coconut milk kefir because the grains are activated in cow's milk.

Ingredients:

1 to 2 tablespoons of kefir grains

2 cups coconut milk

Directions:

If the kefir grains are new grains you just purchased, activate them by placing them in a glass of cow's milk for 24 hours. Strain them out and place them in a fresh glass of cow's milk once 24 hours have passed. Continue straining the kefir grains from the previous day's milk and adding them to new milk until the grains are forming kefir from the milk you're putting them in.

Depending on how strong the kefir grains are, add 1 to 2 tablespoons of kefir grains to 2 cups of coconut milk. Wait for 24 hours and check the milk to make sure it's thickened. Strain out the grains and place the coconut milk kefir in a bottle in the fridge.

If the first batch of coconut milk kefir doesn't turn out the way you expected it to, don't worry. Kefir grains can take a few batches to grow acclimated to a change in the type of milk they're used in. Keep making batches until the kefir is to your liking.

If the coconut milk hasn't thickened within 48 hours, throw the batch out and start again. Strain the grains out and use them to make a new batch.

Fruity Kefir Milk

Fruit juice can be used to flavor kefir *after* it's done fermenting. Make sure the kefir grains have been removed from the milk before you add the juice or you run the risk of destroying the grains. The more fruit juice you add to the kefir, the thinner the flavored kefir milk will be.

Ingredients:

2 cups fresh milk kefir

1/8 cup fruit juice

Directions:

Combine the fruit juice and milk kefir in a glass jar. Place the lid on the jar and shake it until the juice and the kefir are blended. Taste it and add more juice, if necessary.

Fresh Fruit Kefir Smoothies

Blend fresh fruit with milk kefir and what do you get?

A tasty and lightly carbonated smoothie.

This section covers a handful of fresh fruit combinations. Don't be afraid to try your own. In order to make a fresh fruit kefir smoothie, combine 1 cup of kefir milk with as much fresh fruit as you'd like and blend it together in the blender with a handful of ice cubes.

Here are some of my favorite kefir smoothie blends:

- **Strawberry citrus.** 2 tablespoons lime juice, 1 tablespoon lemon juice, 10 strawberries.
- **Strawberry banana.** 1 banana, 5 strawberries.
- **Orange Froth.** 1 cup orange juice, 1 teaspoon vanilla.
- **Tropical blend.** 1 cup pineapple chunks, ½ a mango, ¼ cup coconut milk
- **Pina colada.** ½ cup pineapple chunks, ½ cup shredded coconut.
- **Berry blast.** 15 blueberries, 15 blackberries.

Kefir Soda

These tasty beverages combine cream, kefir and flavored syrup to create a drink that's both delicious and good for you at the same time. Kids love kefir soda, especially if you top it with whipped cream instead of half and half.

Ingredients:

1 cup fizzy milk kefir

Flavored syrup, to taste

1 cup ice

½ cup half and half

Directions:

Place the ice in a glass. Pour the flavored syrup over the ice. You can use whatever flavor of syrup you'd like. Fruit syrups work well in this recipe. Add as much as you'd like, but don't overdo it. You want the flavor to be subtle, as opposed to overpowering.

Fill the rest of the cup with fizzy milk kefir and top it off with an inch or two of half and half. Drink immediately.

Chocolate Kefir

Ingredients:

2 cups fresh milk kefir

2 tablespoons cocoa powder

1 teaspoon raw honey

Directions:

Stir the cocoa powder and raw honey into 2 cups of fresh kefir milk. Serve cold.

Vanilla Almond Kefir

This is one of my favorite kefir recipes. You can also use almond extract or vanilla extract individually to create almond or vanilla kefir milk, respectively. Again, be sure to remove the kefir grains before adding anything to the kefir.

Ingredients:

2 cups fresh milk kefir

1 teaspoon vanilla extract

½ teaspoon almond extract

2 teaspoons raw honey or maple syrup

Directions:

Stir the vanilla extract, almond extract and sweetener into 2 cups of fresh kefir milk. Serve cold.

Kefir Cream Cheese

Cream cheese can easily be made from milk kefir by straining the kefir through a piece of cloth. This cultured cream cheese can be used to replace regular cream cheese in most recipes that call for cream cheese. It also makes a great dip or spread.

Ingredients:

3 cups milk kefir

Directions:

Take a piece of muslin cloth and lay it in a large bowl. Place the 3 cups of milk kefir in the bowl on top of the cloth. Pull all four corners of the cloth up toward the middle to create a bag that contains the kefir. Tie the bag off at the top with a long string.

Hang the bag somewhere warm. Place a bowl underneath it to catch any liquid that drips from the bag. Leave the bag hanging for 24 hours. The curds left inside the bag will be cream cheese. You can eat it as-is or it can be used to cook with. Don't discard the contents of the bowl. This is *whey*. It's packed full of probiotic cultures and can be used as a starter culture for fermenting all sorts of foods.

Place the whey in a clean container and the cream cheese in a separate container and store both in the fridge until you're ready to use them.

Milk Kefir with Fresh Raspberries

This recipe calls for fresh raspberries, but any kind of edible berry will work. Blackberries and blueberries also go well with kefir. Either fresh or frozen berries can be used.

Ingredients:

2 cups fresh milk kefir

1 cup frozen raspberries

1 tablespoon lemon zest

1 tablespoon agave nectar

Directions:

Place the milk kefir in a bowl. Stir the berries into it. Sprinkle the lemon zest on top. Drizzle agave nectar over the top.

Additional Ways to Use Milk Kefir

Milk kefir is used in all sorts of recipes and dishes. It can be used as a replacement for buttermilk and yogurt and kefir cream cheese can be used in place of regular cream cheese. Here are some of the many ways milk kefir can be used:

- **Add fruit to it and eat it.**
- **Add it to a cold soup.**
- **Add it to cereal instead of milk.**
- **Drink it.**
- **Drizzle it over salad.**
- **Make milkshakes with it.**
- **Make pasta sauce with it.**
- **Mix it with ice cream.**
- **Use it as a starter culture for other ferments.**
- **Use it to help leaven bread.**

Use your imagination. I'm constantly coming up with new ways to use milk kefir. Some work great; others not so much, but it's a great feeling when you come up with a winner.

Water Kefir

Water kefir is similar to milk kefir, in that it's a lacto-fermented probiotic beverage made using kefir grains packed with healthy bacteria and yeast, but this kefir drink is largely dairy-free. It can be made from juice, coconut water or pretty much any beverage that contains enough sugar in it for the kefir to thrive.

A single water kefir grain can contain more than 400 different strains of probiotic bacteria and yeast. Just like with milk kefir grains, water kefir grains can be used again and again to create new batches of water kefir. As long as you don't starve them of food for too long or do something that kills the cultures, you'll be able to continuously make new batches of water kefir with your grains.

Water kefir is usually made through a *dual-fermentation process*. In the first fermentation, which lasts 24 to 48 hours, the kefir grains are left in the water. The second fermentation is usually done without the grains and lasts another 24 to 48 hours. The purpose of the second fermentation is to add carbonation to the water kefir. If you're happy with the carbonation level after the first fermentation, you can drink the kefir without fermenting it a second time.

Water kefir recipes call for large amounts of sugar. Sugar is what feeds the kefir and there will be a lot less sugar in the final product than what you poured into the container. The longer the kefir ferments, the less sugar there will be. Fermenting for a day will give you sweet kefir. Ferment for longer than a day and the sweetness slowly but surely fades away as the kefir consumes the sugar in the container. After a 48-hour ferment, water kefir will contain only 20 to 30 percent of the sugar you put into it. The quarter cup you put in will be reduced to less than a tablespoon by the time the water kefir is done fermenting.

As far as alcohol goes, there is some alcohol found in water kefir, but it's fairly low when sugar water is used. Normal sugar water ferments where ¼ cup of white sugar is used will typically have less than 1% alcohol in the final product. This percentage goes up when fruit juices high in sugar are used or if you add more than ¼ cup of sugar to the water.

When properly fed, water kefir grains will sometimes multiply rapidly. Having more grains in your water kefir won't hurt the quality of the kefir, but at some point, you're going to have to remove some of the grains in order to make more room for water. 2 to 3 tablespoons of grains is all you need to make a couple quarts of water kefir at a time. Anything more than that is overkill and may result in your grains starving and becoming unhealthy. Remove the extra grains from the mix and either give them away or dehydrate them and save them in case you need them later.

Don't worry too much if your kefir grains don't multiply. That's normal, too. As long as your grains are making good kefir, they're probably in good health.

When choose water for your kefir, it's best to use clean water that's as free of contaminants as possible. This rules out using tap water in some areas unless it's been filtered. If you're using water that's low in mineral content like reverse osmosis-filtered or distilled water, try adding a pinch of sea salt to it to add back some of the minerals.

Water containing fluoride, chloramines or chlorine can kill probiotic bacteria and should be avoided. You can get rid of chlorine by letting chlorinated water sit overnight. Fluoride has to be filtered out using a filtration method capable of removing fluoride.

Simple Water Kefir

Water kefir is easy to make. All you need is water kefir grains, sugar, water and a non-reactive container to ferment the water kefir in.

Ingredients:

2 tablespoons water kefir grains

¼ cup unprocessed white sugar

4 cups filtered water

Directions:

Heat ½ cup of water and stir the sugar into it while it's warm. Continue stirring until the sugar has dissolved. Pour the warm water into a glass container and add the rest of the water to it. Let the water cool to room temperature.

Add the kefir grains and cover the jar with cheesecloth or a towel. Tie it in place, so it won't come off easily. Let the container sit at room temperature for 1 to 2 days. Once the kefir ferments to your liking, strain the grains out and place a tight lid on the container. If you're going to add flavor to the kefir, add it before you place the lid on container.

Let the kefir sit at room temperature for another day or two before drinking it. You can move it to the fridge if you want chilled kefir, but you don't have to store water kefir in the fridge.

Fizzy Water Kefir

Fizzy water kefir is almost as easy to make as regular water kefir. All it requires is one additional step. If you're familiar with the regular water kefir recipe, all you have to do is make regular water kefir and then place the finished kefir in an airtight container at room temperature for a couple days.

Ingredients:

2 tablespoons water kefir grains

¼ cup unprocessed white sugar

4 cups filtered water

Directions:

Heat ½ cup of water and stir the sugar into it while it's warm. Continue stirring until the sugar has dissolved. Pour the warm water into a glass container and add the rest of the water to it. Let the water cool to room temperature.

Add the kefir grains and cover the jar with cheesecloth or a towel. Tie it in place, so it won't come off easily. Let the container sit at room temperature for 1 to 2 days. Once the kefir ferments to your liking, strain the grains out and place a tight lid on the container.

Don't leave the grains in the water for more than 48 hours, as the grains will be damaged if they run out of food. If you're going to add flavor to the kefir, add it before you place the lid on container.

Let the kefir sit at room temperature for several days. Remove the lid every couple of days to release any pressure that builds up in the container. Be careful when opening the container because the pressure can cause the lid to fly off when you unscrew it. Check the water kefir periodically to see if it has enough fizz. Once it has enough fizz, move it to the fridge to slow the fermentation process or drink it right away.

Cream Soda Kefir

This recipe is for the cream soda lovers out there. This subtly-carbonated cream soda kefir recipe is better than any store-bought cream soda I've ever tried. Except maybe for Boylan's, but this recipe has less sugar and is completely natural.

Ingredients:

2 tablespoons water kefir grains

¼ cup unprocessed white sugar

4 cups filtered water

1 tablespoon vanilla extract

Directions:

Follow the instructions to make simple water kefir. After the kefir has started to ferment, strain out the grains and move the kefir to a glass bottle.

Add the vanilla extract to the kefir. Do not add it before you've removed the kefir grains. It's best to add it after the grains have been removed.

If you're happy with the level of carbonation in the cream soda kefir, cap the bottle tightly and move it to the fridge. If you want more carbonation, cap the bottle and let it sit at room temperature for another day or two before moving it to the fridge.

Water Kefir Lemonade

This is one of my personal favorite water kefir recipes. It's great to sip on during a hot summer afternoon. Put it on ice and enjoy this mildly fizzy lemonade as you cool down and unwind.

Ingredients:

2 tablespoons water kefir grains

¼ cup unprocessed white sugar

4 cups filtered water

¾ cup fresh lemon juice

Directions:

Heat half a cup of water and stir the sugar into it. Add the sugar water and the rest of the filtered water to a glass container and stir the sugar water in. Add the water kefir grains and stir it up some more. The grains will not dissolve into the water.

Cover the jar loosely and let it sit at room temperature for up to 48 hours. The longer you let it sit, the more fizz the kefir will have. Remove the grains from the water before reaching the 48-hour mark.

Add the lemon juice and stir it in. Place a lid on the container and screw it down tightly. If you're happy with the kefir lemonade, you can move the container to the fridge. If you want it fizzier, leave the container at room temperature for another 24 to 48 hours. Open the container at least once a day to off-gas the carbon dioxide created via the fermentation process.

Fruit Juice Kefir

Water kefir can be made by fermenting fruit juice. The best juices to use for fruit juice kefir are juices that are naturally high in sugar and are relatively low in acid. Citrus juices and other high-acid juices should be avoided because they can damage the kefir grains. Fruit juices that are high in sugar will develop into kefir with higher alcohol content than those made with lesser amounts of sugar and water.

To use fruit juices that are high in acid, wait until the kefir grains have been removed after the first fermentation and add the juices for the second fermentation.

Ingredients:

2 to 3 tablespoons water kefir grains

4 cups organic fruit juice

Directions:

Place the water kefir grains and organic fruit juice into a glass container. Place a loose cover on the container and let it sit at room temperature for 24 to 48 hours.

Strain out the kefir grains and move the kefir to a glass bottle. If you want more carbonation in your fruit juice kefir, tightly cap the bottle and leave it at room temperature for another day or two. When you're happy with the carbonation level, drink the fruit juice kefir or move it to the fridge to slow the fermentation process.

Be aware that long fermentation times with fruit juice can result in elevated levels of alcohol in the kefir. Keeping the fermentation periods short should keep alcohol content in fruit juice kefir to less than 1% alcohol by volume.

Berry Kefir

This kefir is for the berry lovers in your family. If you love berries, this is the water kefir recipe for you!

Ingredients:

2 tablespoons water kefir grains

¼ cup unprocessed white sugar

4 cups filtered water

5 blueberries

5 blackberries

2 strawberries

5 raspberries

Directions:

Follow the directions to make simple water kefir. Let the kefir ferment for 24 hours. Strain out the water kefir grains. Add the berries to the container and place a tight lid on it. Let the kefir sit for an additional 24 to 48 hours for the second fermentation.

When you're happy with the ferment, move the water kefir to a glass bottle and move it to the fridge to slow the fermentation process.

Dr. Kefir

In a previous unhealthy life, I was a huge fan of Dr. Pepper. This recipe isn't exactly like Dr. Pepper, but it's close enough to ease the cravings whenever I find myself craving a Dr. Pepper.

Ingredients:

2 tablespoons water kefir grains

¼ cup unprocessed white sugar

4 cups filtered water

1 cup prune juice

¼ cup raisins

Directions:

Follow the directions to make simple water kefir. Let the kefir ferment for 24 hours. Strain out the water kefir grains and move the kefir to a glass bottle.

Add 1 cup of prune juice and ¼ cup raisins to the bottle. Cap the bottle tightly and let it sit at room temperature for another 24 to 48 hours for the second fermentation. Remove the lid once every 12 or so hours to let the gases escape from the bottle. Once you're happy with the carbonation level, strain out the raisins and move the kefir to the fridge to slow the fermentation process.

Cherry Lime Kefir

This is a great water kefir recipe for the kids in your family. If you're concerned about the alcohol in the kefir, skip the second ferment. It'll have a small amount of alcohol in it, but should be less than 1 percent.

Ingredients:

2 tablespoons water kefir grains

¼ cup unprocessed white sugar

4 cups filtered water

10 cherries

2 limes

Directions:

Follow the directions to make simple water kefir. Let the kefir ferment for 24 hours. Strain out the water kefir grains and move the kefir to a glass bottle.

Cut the cherries in half and place them in the bottle. Juice the limes and add the lime juice to the bottle. Tightly cap the bottle and let it ferment for an additional 24 hours at room temperature.

Drink immediately or open the lid to off-gas the carbonation and move the water kefir to the fridge until you're ready to drink it.

Kombucha Tea

Kombucha tea is a fermented sweet tea made from kombucha cultures. Fans of kombucha tea refer to the cultures as "shroomies" or "SCOBY." SCOBY is an acronym for *symbiotic culture of bacteria and yeast.* Kombucha cultures aren't an actual mushroom, but they sometimes resemble one in shape and size.

Kombucha cultures contain one or more yeasts that produce alcohol. The alcohol is then processed into acetic acid by the bacteria residing in the culture. This results in a fermented tea beverage that's low in alcohol and high in acetic acid. The combination of acetic acid and small amounts of alcohol create a sterile environment in which good bacteria can thrive and bad bacteria aren't able to effectively reproduce.

This vinegar-like tea usually has less than half of one percent alcohol content by volume, which allows it to be classified as a non-alcoholic beverage. Allowing kombucha tea to ferment for more than a couple days can up the alcohol content in the tea to between 1% and 2%.

Health Benefits

There hasn't been a whole lot of research done into kombucha tea, but that hasn't stopped its very vocal fans from making a number of claims regarding the health benefits. Here are some of the many health benefits thought to be associated with drinking kombucha:

- **Allergy relief.**
- **Better eyesight.**
- **Detoxification of the body.**
- **Digestive aid.**
- **Elevated energy levels.**
- **Feelings of well-being.**
- **Helps ward off yeast infections.**
- **High in antioxidants and polyphenols.**
- **Increased metabolism.**
- **Immune system boost.**
- **It's packed with probiotic bacteria.**
- **May help prevent cancer.**
- **Sleep aid.**

The probiotic cultures found in kombucha tea are believed to help establish healthy levels of good bacteria in your digestive tract.

Like any drink packed full of probiotic bacteria, kombucha isn't for everyone. It's a powerful tea that can interact with certain prescription medications, so consult with your physician before adding it to your diet. There are also known cases where allergic reactions to kombucha tea have taken place, so proceed with caution.

The benefits individuals gain from kombucha varies from person to person. Each person has a different bacterial composition in their digestive system, which means their body will react differently to the consumption of this tea.

Brewing Kombucha

There are two basic methods used to brew kombucha tea:

- **Batch brewing.**
- **Repeat brewing.**

Batch brewing creates each new batch of kombucha from scratch every time it's made. A container of sweet tea is made and the SCOBY is added to the batch, which is then left to sit for a week or so until the tea ferments into kombucha tea. *Repeat brewing* takes a currently brewed batch of kombucha and adds a small amount of sweet tea to it. The sweet tea is dispersed into the current batch and is quickly fermented, usually within a day or two of having been added.

We'll cover both methods of brewing kombucha tea. Batch brewing obviously has to be used for brewing the first batch of kombucha tea—unless you know someone willing to spare a few cups of tea. After that, it's up to you whether you want to batch brew or repeat brew your kombucha. There are benefits to both.

Let's take a closer look at each of the methods.

Batch-Brewed Kombucha Tea

This method of brewing kombucha tea assumes you're starting from scratch and don't have any previously-brewed kombucha tea on hand. This recipe will make approximately a gallon of tea.

Ingredients:

4 bags of your favorite green or black tea

1 cup organic cane sugar

¼ cup vinegar.

8 cups of filtered water

Kombucha starter culture

Directions:

Wash your hands with apple cider vinegar. Don't use antibacterial hand wash or soap because it can interfere with the bacteria in kombucha.

Place the water in a pot over high heat. Bring the water to a boil and let it boil for at least 5 minutes. Turn off the heat and immediately place the tea bags in the water. Add the sugar to the water and stir it in.

Wait for the tea to cool to room temperature and pour the tea into a glass jar. Add the vinegar to the tea. If you have access to kombucha tea that hasn't been pasteurized or otherwise processed, you can use a cup of the tea instead. The vinegar (or tea) is necessary to get the pH of the tea low enough to prevent bad bacteria or mold from developing.

Add the kombucha SCOBY (starter culture) to the tea. Avoid directly touching it if at all possible. Cover the top of the jar with cheesecloth or cloth and band it or tie it down.

Place the jar somewhere dark and warm. The ideal temperature range is 80 degrees F to 87 degrees F. Avoid fermenting kombucha at temperatures below 70 degrees F because bad bacteria, mold and pathogens are more likely to form.

Let the tea ferment for 7 days. The SCOBY culture may float to the top during the fermentation process. This is fine. Baby SCOBY will typically form at the surface of the kombucha, eventually forming a new SCOBY that acts as a protective barrier. Dip a straw into the tea and block the straw off with your finger to trap tea inside. You can either taste the tea to see if it tastes like vinegar or check the pH to see if it's around 3. If it tastes too sweet or the pH is above 3, more brewing time is needed.

Remove the mother culture and any smaller SCOBY cultures that may have formed and place them in a clean non-reactive container. Cover them with kombucha to keep them safe.

Move the finished kombucha tea to glass containers and place a lid on them. If you're happy with the carbonation level of the kombucha, loosely cap the containers. On the other hand, if you want more carbonation, tightly cap the containers. Let the kombucha ferment for another 3 to 5 days before either drinking it or moving it to the fridge to slow the fermentation process.

Periodically open the container to allow gases trapped inside to escape.

Repeat-Brewed Kombucha Tea

This method of brewing kombucha tea is easier than the batch-brewing method.

In order to repeat brew kombucha tea, you wait until your container of kombucha tea is a quarter of the way empty and refill it with sweet tea. Make sure the sweet tea has cooled to room temperature before adding it to the kombucha. This allows you to continuously feed the kombucha cultures in the tea, keeping the fermenting process going indefinitely.

The SCOBY is left in the kombucha tea container when this method is used. You don't have to transfer it to a glass container and try to keep it healthy in between batches. You can grow a giant SCOBY packed full of beneficial bacteria that will quickly ferment the sweet tea that's added to the container. Instead of having to wait weeks for a new batch, the method cuts the fermenting time down to a day or two. If you have a couple containers, you'll have a constant supply of kombucha.

If you use a container with a spigot, you can easily dispense kombucha directly from the fermenting container. This minimizes the risk of contamination because you're never coming in direct contact with the SCOBY or the kombucha in the container.

Ginger Kombucha

Adding ginger to kombucha creates a fizzy kombucha with more carbonation than regular kombucha tends to have. If the taste of ginger in the kombucha doesn't work for you, try adding some citrus juice. Lime or lemon juice adds an interesting flavor that helps mask the ginger.

Ingredients:

4 bags of your favorite green or black tea

1 cup organic cane sugar

1 cup kombucha tea

8 cups of filtered water

SCOBY culture

3 to 4 ginger slices

Directions:

Wash your hands with vinegar. Place the water in a pot on the stove and bring it to a boil. Add the tea bags and turn off the stove. Once the water stops boiling, add the cane sugar and stir it in. Let the tea cool to room temperature.

Remove the tea bags and place the sweet tea in a glass fermenting container. Add the cup of kombucha tea and place the SCOBY in the container with the tea. Cover the container loosely with a piece of cloth and band it, so it won't come off.

Let the tea ferment for 7 days. Remove the SCOBY culture and prepare it for safekeeping or move it to another batch of kombucha. Place the kombucha in bottles with the ginger slices and cap the bottles tightly. Let the bottles sit for another 4 to 5 days. Open the bottle at least once a day to let the gases out or you run the risk of exploding bottles.

Once the carbonation has developed to your liking, move the bottles to the fridge to slow down the fermentation process.

Cinnamon Citrus Kombucha

Cinnamon and orange juice aren't items that usually walk hand-in-hand, but for some reason, they work surprisingly well in kombucha. Some people add turmeric to this recipe, adding even more health benefits to the tea. Turmeric is thought to be good for the heart and has anti-inflammatory properties.

Ingredients:

8 cups kombucha tea

2 tablespoons fresh orange juice

1 teaspoon ground cinnamon

1 teaspoon turmeric (optional)

Directions:

This recipe assumes you've already got kombucha that's been through the first 5- to 7-day ferment. If not, you're going to have to make some. Be sure to remove the SCOBY from the kombucha before adding the ingredients in this recipe. If you're using the repeat brewing method, pour 8 cups of the tea into a separate container before adding the orange juice and spices.

Place the kombucha, orange juice, cinnamon and turmeric into a glass container and stir it all together. Place the lid on the container and let it sit for 3 to 5 days until it's fermented to your liking. Be sure to open the container once a day to allow any gases that have built up to escape. Once the kombucha has fermented to your liking, move the container to the fridge.

Chamomile Kombucha

Chamomile tea is a favorite tea for many because of its relaxing qualities. Chamomile kombucha infuses the flavor of chamomile into kombucha tea to create a relaxing probiotic beverage.

Ingredients:

8 cups kombucha tea

2 tablespoons chamomile

Directions:

This recipe assumes you've already got kombucha that's been through the first 5- to 7-day ferment. If not, you're going to have to make some. Be sure to remove the SCOBY from the kombucha before adding the chamomile. If you're using the repeat brewing method, pour 8 cups of the tea into a separate container before adding the chamomile.

Place the chamomile and kombucha tea into a glass bottle and place the lid on the bottle. Leave it to ferment for 3 to 5 days. Once the chamomile kombucha has fermented to your liking, strain out the chamomile and move the tea to the fridge.

Cucumber Mint Kombucha

This kombucha tea is infused with the flavor of cucumber and mint. It's refreshing and goes down equally smooth as a morning tea or a tea consumed on a hot summer afternoon.

Ingredients:

8 cups kombucha tea

5 slices of cucumber

10 fresh mint leaves

Directions:

This recipe assumes you've already got kombucha that's been through the first 5- to 7-day ferment. If not, you're going to have to make some. Be sure to remove the SCOBY from the kombucha before adding the ingredients in this recipe. If you're using the repeat brewing method, pour the tea into a separate glass brewing container before adding the cucumber and mint leaves.

Lightly bruise the cucumber slices and the mint leaves. Place them in a glass fermenting container and add the kombucha tea to the container. Place a lid on the container and ferment the tea for an additional 3 to 5 days. Once the tea is fermented to your preference, move the container to the fridge.

Kombucha Coffee

This recipe is for those who can't survive without their morning cup of coffee. Now, you can have your coffee while adding probiotic bacteria to your digestive system. It tastes great and gives you a probiotic boost.

Ingredients:

8 cups fresh coffee

½ cup sugar

Kombucha culture

Directions:

Brew the coffee. Stir the sugar into it while it's hot. This may seem like a lot of sugar, but most of it will be processed by the bacteria long before you drink the coffee. The final product will have a fraction of the sugar you put into it.

Let the coffee cool to room temperature and strain it to remove any coffee grounds found in the coffee. Add the coffee to the fermenting container and place the kombucha culture into the coffee.

Cover the container with a piece of cloth and tie or band the cloth to ensure the cover stays on. Let the coffee ferment at room temperature in a warm area of your house for 5 days. Remove the kombucha culture and taste the coffee. Place a lid on the container and let it continue fermenting for up to 5 more days. Taste the coffee regularly and bottle it once it's fermented to your liking. Store the bottles in your fridge.

Serve the kombucha coffee cold. Heating it will kill the probiotic bacteria and render the coffee ineffective. This coffee is good served over ice with cream. It should be sweet enough without having to add additional sugar, but you can if you want to.

What to Do With All Those SCOBYs

Each batch of kombucha will typically develop a new culture at the top of the container. This culture will start off as a thin gelatinous substance that'll soon form into a brand new baby SCOBY. This is exciting the first few times you see it happen, but you may soon find yourself with more kombucha cultures than you know what to do with.

The following list should give you a few ideas of what you can do with the extra "shrooms" you'll end up with if you make kombucha for any extended period of time:

- **Add them to your compost bin.** They'll add beneficial bacteria to your compost bin.
- **Eat them.** That's right. Kombucha SCOBYs are edible and as long as they haven't been allowed to die, they're packed full of probiotic cultures. You aren't going to want to pop one in your mouth and choke it down, but you won't notice the flavor too much if you add it to a smoothie.
- **Feed them to your pets.** Dogs, cats and even chickens all love dried SCOBYs.
- **Give them away.** Spread the wealth, so other people can experience the joys of fermenting their own kombucha.

Kombucha Safety

Properly-brewed kombucha is thought to be safe for most people. That said; problems can occasionally arise during the brewing process that you should be aware of in advance.

First of all, here are a few things that might happen that aren't always indicative of a problem:

- **Brown stringy yeast forms in the water.**
- **The color of the water changes.**
- **The original SCOBY can float, sink or suspend itself somewhere in the middle.**
- **The SCOBY growing on the top suddenly sinks to the bottom.**
- **White sediment forms near the top of the container.**

Mold is the most common problem with kombucha. It typically occurs when the pH in the container isn't acidic enough to ward off foreign cultures. Contaminants left in the brewing container (like coffee grounds or pieces of food) can also introduce mold into kombucha. Mold is more likely to form when fermenting at less than ideal temperatures.

While you may be attached to your kombucha culture, if mold forms during a ferment, you're going to have to throw out the SCOBY and start with a fresh one. Once mold has contaminated the culture, there's no telling what could end up growing in your kombucha in the future.

Old SCOBYs that have been misused or allowed to go without food for long periods of time won't be as effective as cultures that have been kept in good health. They will sometimes darken in color and may even turn black. If this happens, it's time to replace the SCOBY with a new one.

Another common problem with kombucha is flies and other flying insects finding their way inside your container, where they lay eggs that hatch into maggots. This is why it's important to cover the top of the fermenting vessel and to band it or tie it shut tightly. If you find maggots in your kombucha or notice insects flying in and out, discard the contents of the container and start fresh.

If you're fermenting kombucha and no SCOBY forms on the top, you've got a problem. There should be some surface activity. The lack of activity could be due to antibacterial soap being used on the vessel, environmental issues like heat or contaminants or not enough food for the bacteria to grow. Adding spices and other flavoring agents can damage the SCOBY and inhibit growth of bacteria, so it's best to remove the SCOBY before adding anything other than tea and sugar to the mix.

Use your best judgment when determining if kombucha is safe to consume. If something doesn't look, feel or taste right, it probably isn't. It's better to toss a batch out and start over with a new SCOBY than it is to drink tea you aren't sure about and end up sick.

Kvass

Kvass, also known as *kvas* and *quass*, is a traditional Eastern European and Russian beverage made of fermented bread. It's been around since ancient times, with the first known use of the beverage dating back more than a thousand years. Kvass has been a staple ever since, and is now sold by street vendors and supermarkets alike.

There are a number of variants on the traditional kvass recipe, which uses rye bread. It's also made from wheat and barley bread and there are versions of kvass flavored with everything from fruit to tree sap. There's also a popular version of the beverage made from beets and another made using fruit.

Kvass does contain some alcohol, but it's generally less than 1% alcohol by volume. To put it in perspective, a wine cooler usually has at least 4% alcohol.

This fermented beverage is popular in Russia, where kids in the summer flock to vendors selling kvass in the streets. Russian children love it, but your kids probably won't, as it takes a bit of getting used to. Traditional kvass has a strong sour taste that borders on pungent.

Traditional Kvass Recipe

Traditional kvass is prepared with dry rye bread, but you can substitute wheat bread or barley bread in if you have trouble sourcing rye bread. Chop the bread up into small cubes and dry it in the oven for 15 to 20 minutes if you want to store it for more than a couple days.

Ingredients:

10 cups water

1 pound crumbled black bread (rye bread)

½ cup sugar

1 teaspoon dry yeast

A handful of raisins

Mint leaves (optional)

Directions:

Chop the rye bread up and dry it out by placing it in the oven for at least 15 minutes. Cook the bread until it's completely dried out and has little moisture left.

Place the water in a large pot and bring it to a boil. Place the bread in a glass bowl and pour the boiling water over the top of the bread. Place a piece of cloth or a towel over the bowl and let it sit for 3 to 4 hours in a cool place.

Stir the sugar into the bread and water mixture. Combine the dry yeast with 5 tablespoons of warm water and mix it together. Pour the yeast water into the bread and water mixture and stir it in. Cover the bowl with a cloth or a towel and let it sit in a warm area of the house to ferment for 12 hours.

Strain the kvass through at least 2 pieces of cheesecloth stacked on top of one another. If there are particles floating in the kvass after the first time you strain it, strain it again. Pour the kvass into non-reactive bottles. Leave an inch or two of headspace at the top of the bottle. Add a few raisins to each container and cap the bottle. Add a mint leaf to each bottle, if you'd like.

Let the kvass sit at room temperature for 4 to 6 hours and move it to the fridge. Remove the lid periodically to let out any gases that may build up.

Fruit Kvass

Fruit kvass really only shares a name with traditional kvass. It's a fermented fruit drink that forgoes the rye bread and uses ripe fruit instead. It's an effervescent beverage that's fairly low in alcohol. Most fruit kvass measures in at less than 1% alcohol by volume.

Ingredients:

8 to 10 cups filtered water

Organic fruit

1 tablespoon shredded ginger

1 tablespoon unprocessed sugar

3 tablespoons whey (optional)

Directions:

Place ginger into a large glass jar. Add the water and stir in the sugar. Add the whey now if you're planning on using it. It'll help start the fermenting process, but usually isn't necessary.

The following fruits work well for fruit kvass:

- **Apples (sliced).**
- **Apricots (halved).**
- **Blackberries.**
- **Blueberries.**
- **Cherries (halved).**
- **Lemons (sliced).**
- **Mangoes (sliced).**
- **Peaches and nectarines (halved or sliced).**

- **Raisins.**
- **Raspberries.**
- **Strawberries (halved).**

Pick a fruit or any combination of fruit you like and add it to the jar. You can also try adding vegetables and herbs and spices to create interesting flavor combinations. The possibilities are endless.

Place a lid tightly on the jar and let the contents ferment at room temperature for a couple days. Mix the contents of the jar up once a day.

The fruit kvass is done when there are carbonation bubbles floating to the top and the kvass tastes tangy. This usually takes a couple days at room temperature, but needs to be monitored closely because it can happen faster. Once the kvass has fermented to your liking, strain out the fruit and store the kvass in sealed glass containers in the fridge.

Beet Kvass

Beet kvass is a tradition Russian beverage that manages to be both salty and tangy at the same time. Beets are packed with vitamins, minerals and antioxidants, so it's no surprise this drink is considered a probiotic powerhouse. It also looks amazing, since the beets impart their bright red color to the liquid.

Ingredients:

2 beets

3 cups fresh beet juice

Starter culture

1 tablespoon unrefined sea salt

Directions:

Wash the beets and peel them. Cut them into 1" cubes. Place the beets in the fermenting container. Add the beet juice to the container. Fill it to within a few inches of the top of the jar.

Add the starter culture and sea salt. ¼ cup of whey works well for this recipe. Place a weight in the container and press it down on top of the beets. Place a piece of cheesecloth over the top of the container and let it sit at room temperature for a couple days. The kvass is done when it starts to bubble. You should see little white bubbles on top of the liquid within a couple days.

Once the kvass starts bubbling, move it to the fridge. You can remove the beets and reuse them to make another batch of kvass if you'd like. The second batch won't be as strong as the first, but it'll still be pretty good.

EDITOR'S NOTE: This recipe is from the first book in this series, "Fermenting: How to Ferment Vegetables," by the same author. If you're interested in fermenting vegetables, here's a link to the book:

http://www.amazon.com/Fermenting-How-Ferment-Vegetables-ebook/dp/B00EKN7VS2/

Fermented Sodas

Making fermented sodas is extremely easy.

The only ingredients you have to have on hand are sugar, water and the culture you plan on using. This creates an environment in which fermentation can take place. While these three ingredients are all you absolutely need, fermented sugar water isn't exactly the most appealing beverage on its own. It's OK, but there are so many other things you can do with fermented soda that I don't think you'll want to settle for plain fermented soda water.

The following steps cover the soda fermentation process required to make 1 gallon of soda:

1. Add 8 cups of water to a pot and bring it to a boil.
2. Stir 1 ½ cups of sugar into the boiling water. Rice malt, rapadura and maple sugar all work well. Honey should be avoided because it is antibacterial by nature. If you want to add honey, add it after fermentation has occurred.
3. Boil the liquid until it thickens into syrup.
4. Add the syrup and the remaining 8 cups of water to the fermentation container. Wait for the mixture to cool to room temperature.
5. Add 1 cup of starter culture to the container.
6. Add flavoring at this time and cover the container. If you want highly carbonated soda, seal the container so it's airtight. If the container

is sealed, it's going to need to be opened at least once a day to allow gases that build up to escape.

7. Let the soda ferment at room temperature for at least 5 days. Check it after 5 and if it's too sweet or you want more carbonation, let it ferment for longer.

8. Filter out any particles or fruit and place the soda in bottles and seal the bottles tightly. Wait another couple days to allow carbonation to build up.

9. Move the bottles to the fridge once they're carbonated to your liking. This will slow fermentation to a crawl.

Any of the following ingredients can be added to fermented sodas for flavoring:

- **Flavored syrups.**
- **Fruit.**
- **Ginger.**
- **Herbs and spices.**
- **Honey (add at end of fermentation).**
- **Juice (use fresh-squeezed juices).**
- **Mint.**
- **Peppermint.**
- **Prune juice.**
- **Raisins.**
- **Roots.**
- **Sarsaparilla and sassafras (to make root beer).**
- **Spearmint.**
- **Vanilla extract (to make cream soda).**

Mix and match ingredients to suit your taste. Half the fun of making fermented sodas is experimenting with the many possible ingredients and seeing what you can come up with.

Contact the Author

I sincerely hope you enjoyed this book and are able to make use of the tips, techniques and recipes contained herein. I'd love to hear from you. If you have additional tips, techniques or recipes you'd like to see in future iterations of the book, send me an e-mail at the following address:

mike_rashelle@yahoo.com

I'll get back to you as soon as possible.

Other Books You May Be Interested In

The book you just read is the second book in the *fermenting* series. Here's the first book:

http://www.amazon.com/Fermenting-How-Ferment-Vegetables-ebook/dp/B00EKN7VS2/

Essential oils are the concentrated essence of plants. Learn all about their many therapeutic qualities in the following book.

The Aromatherapy & Essential Oils Handbook

http://www.amazon.com/dp/B00BECCJXY

Diet plays a huge role in healthy living. If you're interested in healthy eating, there are a number of healthy foods you may be interested in adding to your diet. The following books may be of interest to you.

The Coconut Flour Cookbook: Delicious Gluten Free Coconut Flour Recipes

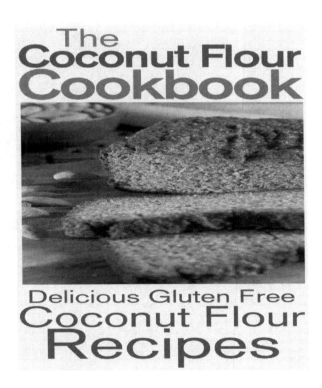

http://www.amazon.com/dp/B00CC0JFPM

**The Almond Flour Cookbook: 30 Delicious and
Gluten Free Recipes**

http://www.amazon.com/dp/B00CB3SJ0M

The Quinoa Cookbook: Healthy and Delicious Quinoa Recipes (Superfood Cookbooks)

http://www.amazon.com/dp/B00B2T2420

The Coconut Oil Guide: How to Stay Healthy, Lose Weight and Feel Good through Use of Coconut Oil

http://www.amazon.com/The-Coconut-Oil-Guide-ebook/dp/B00CESE3HC/

Made in the USA
Middletown, DE
08 July 2015